COWBOY

CW00956948

Also by Kandace Siobhan Walker

COWBOY

KANDACE SIOBHAN WALKER

CHEERIO

First published in Great Britain in 2023
by CHEERIO Publishing
www.cheeriopublishing.com
info@cheeriopublishing.com

10 9 8 7 6 5 4 3 2 1

Typeset in Perpetua by Martha Sprackland
for CHEERIO Publishing

Printed and bound by TJ Books Ltd, Padstow, Cornwall.

A CIP catalogue record for this book is available
from the British Library.

ISBN: 978 1 80081 814 9

Contents

small horses ride me
carry my dreams
of prairies and frontiers
where once
the first people roamed
claimed union with the earth
no right to own or possess

bell hooks

I been in the valley, you ain't been up off that porch now

Lil Nas X

COWBOY

Wales / You! Me! Dancing!

Meet me at the station. Shotgun front seat.
Dreams and lads in the hedgerows, the past
is only ever the past. Driving with the windows down.
Nostalgia's campesinos call my name only when we're alone.
I'm like rain – I decide when I've come home.
The past is a colourised movie. I'm proud but I would eat
every sound and shadow for a foothold.
We're all ashamed of what we want: a blue tick,
nationalism, a view from the sunroof.
I want to feel human. To belong to other people is
to want other people to belong to you.

Mustang

The canyon rainfalls are baboons with roses.
Nighttime's religious core is wherever you
touch me; I'm absolutely dolphins. I'm molten.
If we fall in love, the world. The gorgeous
world. For my stained glass mattress,
we invent east, then west. Fuck, I'm chameleons
about your lips, your sainted fingers –
I'm asking you to leave. Before I'm blue mountain bats,
before water returns to the rivers, before we are
rocking chairs at dawn.   Spare me,
while we're still four-legged, hoofed and wild.

Niagara Barrel Blue

Fell through the mist of a waterfall prismatic,
the way a baby plunges through the christening bowl,
landing in the river where doctors with eager crowbars
unsealed my head and let out all my crazy seawater.
I'd asked to be sent down in a barrel, had wanted
the medical to pry me away from living

with my eye pressed to the bunghole.
I was diagnosed as being a real desperado,
performing the high wire of
facial expressions between skyscrapers,
the flaming tricycle of emotional dysregulation,
even the disfluent choreography of speech,
and hiding, where I could, the drowning
magician of my affect, the crushed plastic
casket of electrical humming. I ran from

the frank rock face of unscripted conversations,
kissed the airbag of tongueless
wish-making. Before, I was as scattered and blue
as distance, now psychiatry wanted to fill me
with the clear, compliant beauty of glass fixed
to tin salt and silver and fool's gold.
But the reflection held nothing

beyond an idea of knowledge.
Kneeling at the root of light, in the bore of myself,
my personality's springtime was as alien as
the evening I walked into emergency

with a dream of the valley beating in my wrists.
The daredevil keeps rehearsing a fall
to meet the sky, until she can swim the mystery
of both its real colour and its twin shade:
miles of ocean, lips moving without sound.

Prism

Board trustees tapped heirloom spoons against the graduates'
wet green skulls to get at the yolk. Academics, in chorus,
drilled and blew until we were bright   and
airy,   ready for democracy.   Cheeks inflated like
   bubonic plague,
foreheads stretched like   drumskin, rainbowed
like wounds, skin   whining, funny helium voices.
I watched the best essayists of my generation float
over the Amazon   rainforest and burning   California
to drink the sun from the sky,   bite and chew and beat its
   yellow,
so they came back to us   rigged, rainless sierras.
Each time we fell to the ground like flies
under an educative glass,   never realising
some skies have a limit, and this is ours.

7

California

Dreamt I had a nom de guerre. Someone was hawking
The OC season three at a junkyard sale.
Love is very rare, but box sets are as common
as grey whales. I went fishing
in my crush's pupils. Every white sail
flew over the summer trees like a state funeral,
like wind, like ribbon dancers surrendering
the last day of term. We waited for the bus
in a silence that knew what it wanted.
My crush asked if I had any mints. But I did not.

Miss Diagnosis

What happens is, she freezes when her mascara runs under
    the beauty lights' migraine aura –
halo for the saint of overwhelm – and her line escapes,
the hush of her
eyeshadowed, hand on hip, swimsuit sensory, medicated
    and masking
– a script against sudden colour, traffic of sound and
movement, self
unwelcome within its self – realises the grief and lateness
of a birth, of misdiagnosis, a grief
as hyper-experiential as a kaleidoscope.
The catwalk tears apart, the audience's unmethodical faces
slumping into shadows; flowers, maybe, or fruit, redolent
    or putrid,
cast at her feet
like gavels; the heckles as midnight, as applause.

But it's commonly nighttime where she grew up,
like many losers of a race not yet called, and she's thinking
    about her parents'
kitchen cabinets, where, selectively mute, she hid, breathing
    as quiet
as dreaming of even a square of blue sky, a falling leaf –
    the way she held out for a green and rising self-discovery.
And the contestant, blinking the way she practised –
small and social in eveningwear's lying, phatic pearls –
repeats what she just said
about world peace, then, exhausted, slips the mirror,

her public face's pageantry gathering around her ankles.
Turning, like a pattern of jewels, petals and leaves,
away from the judges' scorecards, she calls backstage:
I know you're there, you can come out now.

What If I Walked into a Bar and Was Served by a Horse,

after Ada Limón and Brother Blue

saloon doors musical in the wake of my entrance, because in this joke I am the western wind, fond of rye whiskey and a folktale; what if no hush fell over the other patrons, the room uninterested, unthreatened – if this were a more generous landscape – what if we were all emperors and river dragons with true names; what if you were the person who loved me, or what if I was the person you loved; what if who loved me had nothing to do with my horse-ness; what if we were not the people we are, but canyons and bison, or what if I was a real cowboy, what if I loved myself? what if I was content with a night sky and a good tale and my own wild interior and the company of cattle; what if I listened when the moon told the caterpillar, cool it, baby, cool it – just hang – be cool.

Traditional Religion, or, Animism

The sky is upside-down. Forests rain into late summer's
folk religions, recovered from the museum's maw.
We are heathered valleys and masquerade, the griot in
his dry grass cape sings like autumn.
Smells like burnt soap. Tastes like seawater.
We are a ceramic jar
of mythical beasts.

Leaves in perfect definition. Everyone gathers like hands.
    Yes, yes —
every thing has its spirit and this
chorus is a spirit,
which is yes, jealousy, yes,
secrecy, yes, a kind of dying if you want, yes.
Even by telling you this we are breaking our heart open
    like fruit. Yes,
we are forbidden from burying the griot,
yes, we abandon him, curled like a grape leaf inside a
    hollow tree,
the ground, the river, the night, will not have him.
All the forms we took in the forest . . . everything
    the hecatomb knew is gone.
But yes, the sky bites down, yes, we can dance on it,
new men in the trees and it doesn't matter, because yes,
    absolutely, we walk on leaves
with nothing underneath.

Brownie McGhee

Lake Ontario, beach, Mum's braids
whipping the sweat from her shining waist,
baby in the pram, ice cream melting into my heart line.
Years away from independence,
from the years locked inside myself,
a walking radio blackout, dead air.

Evening in town, our legs and laughter
cutting small parcels out of the dark.
At the bank, the banjo-playing clown
sings the blue out of the sky.
Years out from the fall of Rome,
we join him. Together, play the day out.

Snakeskin

Let me know the taste
on the street   where I was
Let me know the cool
down by where
Let me know the deep
where my father was born.
we have,
The more
the more
The less we will know.
So little salt
So far, so
whip-crack
Turn around.
farm animals bray,
a reflection
clouds.
the skin
in rain-softened timber.
something like pressure.
lightning,

of the air
born.
of the sea
my mum was born.
of the earth where
The fewer images
the more we must make.
names we find,
we must seek.
So many curses.
at the door.
far from easy. I want to
overhead.
I want to make
eyes rolling
of storm
I want to burrow below
like wet rot
I want to be
Something like
indivisible.

Astronaut

I want to build a spaceship out of my ex-girlfriend's truck
can you do that I want to write my name on the moon is
this a revenge thing yes the mechanic wipes the oil from
her brow it glistens like snakeskin she says it'll be pricey
I say I am willing to pay anything to stop feeling like this
anywhere you go she says this feeling will follow you well
thank you I say but I do not need a therapist I need a flat-
bed 1965 blue Ford pickup truck fitted with wings and
thrusters and a flux capacitor we'll be working all winter
she says and I say good because working is keeping busy
and that's what my mum says I should do the mechanic
in her denim dungarees tan work boots flannel shirt
creased collar clear plastic safety goggles sharp yellow
sparks erupting from the tools I have neither names nor
qualifications for at the end of every hard day we watch
eighties movies the boy-heroes win popular girls' hearts
by doing terrible things that make us weep I take off my
glasses and ask the mechanic if I am beautiful now she
says, honestly no and we laugh who needs to be pretty
who needs to be loved who needs to be the definition of
love not me some people aren't built for love I tell her but
she shakes her head, you don't believe that's true I do I
say no you don't you believe in the supremacy of emotion
you believe that love sits on the water's surface like the
reflection of the moon I sleep on the mechanic's sofa bed
because I have nowhere to go but up I fall asleep halfway
through the movie I dream my eyes turning to ice outside
my head stars I dream about my ex-girlfriend glancing at
the sky and saying that fucking bitch because there I am

rising like a ghost in the pale noon nobody ever warns you how easily you will abandon yourself and now I am leaving I will miss you sleeping on my sofa the living room will feel small without you it is what it is the rooms always feel smaller the mechanic reminds me that there is no season for spite but I have to do this because my ex said I have no follow-through everything is shaking around me but nothing explodes as I leave the atmosphere into newborn outer space I am the boy-hero my eyeballs blowing up like party balloons the air inside me is trying to escape and expand in the wrong order everybody warned me every-where even in big wide space her face in the continents I'm not built for love for love I can be rebuilt

Suburbia

We're a wet hairdryer full of teenagers. Even the tubaist
knows to keep time with my slow pulse. We're the orchestra.

Tonight's the Big Game, that's what the boys call me.
I want what I don't want, learning to live in the bleachers,

in scratched CDs, on the rough faded carpets we call spring.

His signet ring against her blue Gap skirt,
the arch of my back. Against the bloody stage

velvets I'm brighter than varsity, burning hotter
than a read text. On the playing field, we keep it hush-

hush. I'm dancing in the gallery. Starman said not to play to me.

Chestnut Tree, Wishing Well

What a beautiful day to have a miscarriage!
I wish it was *Daddy, I love him* printed on a T-shirt
but it's a birdsong in the blue morning type of situation,
it's a Billie Holiday dog days of summer cherry Lambrini
pink bubbly vomit type of situation we have here.
Evenings coming up faster now. I take a test.
There's the beginning of you. I bleed
through my pyjamas – there's the end.
In my experience death involves dialling codes
but I call no one, involve no one.
For six weeks I walk around the park feeling
pretend like swans on a manmade lake, so
not good but not worse because I am double-alive,
until a blue line returns me to baseline aliveness.

Neopet

—it's a circle, right? Virtual pet websites are about wealth accumulation. Wealth accumulation is about class. Class is about domination, and domination, of course, is about popular consensus. Popularity is about currency. Currency is points. Points are about buying commodities. Commodities are weapons and armour and property and paintbrushes. Paintbrushes are about customising your Neopet to look like a wizard or a gold bust or a fairy or cloud spirit, but pretty much everyone wants a baby paintbrush. Baby paintbrushes are about making everything really cute. And making everything really cute is just reimagining normal stuff in a palette of pastels and puppy eyes. Puppy eyes are about maternal instinct. Maternal instinct is about the gendered division of labour. The division of labour is about owners and masters. Owners and masters, even when they're six-year-olds, are about capitalism (and its precedents). And capitalism and its precedents are about wealth accumulation, which brings me back to—

Real Person Fanfiction

Ethics are white marble
statues restored to uncomplicated colour.
We made world-order lust from binary
code, absent boundaries.
Masked in gateway fetishes,
real people are modern fruit.
Juice and paint, garden peas.
Especially before rain ruins
the boulevards, the bathtubs are invisible.
Not every love is granted a polis.
You keep only what you can download.

Art of Girlhood

Who is human and who can't be?
The angels ask us who is like God.

The literal translation of my name is light.
I am always looking for meaning somewhere.

Ever seen a blue so deep it was black? Then
you'll recognise the practiced art of absence.

We exceed borders and bandwidth,
we're beyond the imagination of power.

In the bathroom there is always a girl
who will tell me exactly where I was born.

As soon as I heard my bones shift and whine
below the hand of someone I wanted to love,

I knew I'd never seen water for what it really was.
We're persuasive arguments. We're beyond translations.
Don't just ask for it. Thrust your hands in, pull it out.

Gentrifiers

We love the old shows. Power lines, trainers. Pound-a-bowl. We love the views
of the wharf in summer. Chips and mushy peas, hatch on the way home. Who has ever been as
happy as me? Playing sleeping beauties for weeks, while construction crews and green fields
play for keeps. Our heads are like a spindle in the attic.
    We are surrounded by static, film grain before a title screen.
        Heaven is a familiar street in South London,

but we can't keep waking up under rent and fluorescents.
If I know one thing, it's that I know one thing.

The night wants to be alive without risk, to be the mist-like midges swirling
under the streetlamp in the back alley, the shadows in the wings, the band
blooming in the pit, the reflections in the sax's neck, the wild sweat from the conductor's
sober brow, the expectant, submissive audience, their dark theatre, the glittering
circus bulbs lining the marquee of the grand old hippodrome.

Cowboy

I don't wanna be the doctor-son. I wanna walk past the beeping washing machine in rebellion. Every now and then I wanna stop existing.

Just wanna be the prodigal daughter, telephoning to say I'm at arrivals, leaving the bed unmade, watching from the veranda while my siblings

wash the fatted calf's blood out of the wood, only raising a pinkie to drink sweet tea. Supper at the table I call head, you eat when I eat.

Cicadas breathe out the night. I wanna live a life without ambition too. Pink grain and Spanish moss by the roadside. The sky can fuck itself.

Faster Internet at the Reynolds' Plantation

It changes, turning
as violently as thick grey pine
smoke in clearing season.
Tabby foundations, rotting
stilt houses. An overseer's blue book holds
all the passwords. White stone in the summer garden,
misremembering the tobacco king's empty Roman pool.
I want to blog. This is the only computer with email
on the island, my bio-dad explains. I will forget to visit
the unmarked graves. Nowhere is static,
it doesn't change.

Rodeo

Dream-blue and inarticulate in a fringed suede sky,
echoes of the bull's back hooves. Howdy, weirdo!

My play cousins are brawling over the right
way to lose a crab. Two rodeo clowns pry pole stars

from my sweet tea eyelids and peach breath,
amphetamines and floodlights.

The winner's face like a hill of skulls.

Jim Crow's Second-to-Last Waltz

Gallon of rum, I ask the cashier, against trees older than
my ancestry. The filling station painted icy, bridal
white. Too clean to be abandoned. Even the fuel tank,
    white.
Even the gas pump, white. Manhattan was statuary,
but Brooklyn was cool enough to cost anything,
even its warehouses and poverties. Even my beau.
Rum off the highway is twenty dollars. I'm making mojitos.
Too many ghosts here, my girlfriend's white girlfriend says.
Even the slaughtered bark. Tell me how fast a live oak falls,
how long a forest takes to grow.

Historically Accurate Recreation

Land is never ceded willingly,
say the caretakers of this million-dollar slave village.
The village knows the state is the natural enemy
of its descendants. In the square you sit to eat
lunch with the other returnees, under statues
of our ancestors, gold and bronzed in a light that never ends.
After the tour, you are given a deed in our maiden name.
Naturally, all this comes after we have fought and won and
    freed and fed
and clothed and housed every last one of us until we are all
    satisfied,
for a time. You fear the dust will unsettle, and it will. But
    time was that
everything we see was just a petition and a dream.

Sierra

after Jericho Brown

A swimming pond is a national project.
Horse girls are my Mr Hyde.

Police ride horseback through Hyde Park,
like armies training in the trees.

Real life arms and trains me against symmetry.
Politically, I am the object of war.

I am more and more an objection to policy.
Nature exists in opposition to you, not me.

My existence isn't naturally oppositional
but I will always have dark sky status,

and you'll be lurking my statuses in dark mode.
A nation without a heart is a country without lakes.

I will be the heart, the nation, the without, the lakes:
a swimming pond is a national project.

Three Mangoes, £1

You know the dead are never dead / because I saw my
mum's mum / walking down Lewisham High Street / she
was wearing purple / she's always wearing purple / tak-
ing bites out of unripe mangoes / replacing them with the
other fruit / either she was invisible to the market ven-
dors / or unimaginable / the same thing really / our dead
couldn't stay dead even if they wanted to / what we call a
legacy / her voice / when she spoke / sounded tinny with
a hair-raising intimacy // we met last in a Toronto suburb
/ I remember / nothing about her / except pearls, deep
violet dress / full wig of violent / shine curls / her home
smelled like clean magic / fans running in every room /
but she wouldn't open the windows / afraid we'd let the
dead back / in / as if they hadn't made it through cus-
toms in our suitcases / her figure wavered / a telephone
line with a fault / her death too was technical / speaking
nothing of the bloated cancers / marbled purple calves /
decaying waterlogged feet / an email / with her name in
the subject line // just the Barbadian man from Waltham-
stow recognised iron in the air / her smell / like an an-
imal wound / he looked up, put a mango in a wrinkled
blue bag / his smile was not without empathy // for free
/ he said / there's no way to bury these things / earth will
only spit it back out / he must've known / he said eat /
in the park / it's a day / neither fine nor good / just a day

Nationality and Borders

My left cheek kisses the ceiling – my lips breathe under-water. Imperialism is so fucking boring and predictable, it falls to us to strangle class society in its summer bed. Childhood, for me, was watching politicians pry the dio-rama's roof wide, the duvet pulled up to my neck. In that way, it was not a childhood. In that same way, this is not a life. I learned my assumed meaning is division at the air-port – detainment as a dollhouse – five-year-olds filling in landing cards, trying to remember the meaning of 'home' and 'address'. While one does grow weary, I was never un-der any impression that my being was unconditional. My second meaning is to keep kicking, pray we float.

Cleaning Ladies II

History's subjects dream we live without witness. Yellow gloves, bucket and bundled twigs. Vertebrae curved like questions, vacuum cleaners on the commuter train. A client asks what we are, when we are not his. A mirror. Pools of still water, white alloy. Sand. Human shapes with silvered heads. We are romantic: legible as artists, improbable as people. Inscriptions on the monastery wall that tourists won't translate. We register as nothing to men who understand nothing. The receipts for our subjectivity don't cash here in this jungle of self-creation, with its tripwires and ballrooms. When we look up how far can we observe? How opaque the renters' sky. The afterlife and the undercommons. Titans and monsters inhabiting dark continents. The human versus personhood versus animal-man. Hush, the objects of history are deep in meditation. We goeth all naked, so we hear. We goeth in the garden and deep in the abyss. We are the world's farthest edge. Waterfalling into space. See the nebula inside the fraternity of stars? Some apocalypses are necessary: we will be the bloom, you will be the stem. How do we feel? How do we know? How do we be?

Everything and nothing. Awaken!

There Is a Man

Even water buffalo dream. In their creation myth,
the white bird brings down the sky like rain
in her digits. And the sun just keeps rising forever.
For the egrets, the great water buffalo, like a workhorse,
drags the ground away from the lakes so they can land.
Clearly cows are in communication with something
divine. Everything that bathes and wallows, even in mud,
commands an inner life. Underwater light is visible
as tractor beams, pulling up. In the air its true nature
    disappears.
I'm doubtful we invented belief: there's a reason
    gods come down as animals.
Elephants adorn the dead, chimpanzees dance for heavy
    rainfall.
Every one has a language, the failure is ours. It is not only
    biology
why the buffalo taxis the bird around the waterways.
I could argue against human exceptionalism but
even in this title, there is a man. At the end of the world
the egret pulls the sky down again, and there is darkness,
    asking
But what do men know of the world without men?

New Cross

My girls and I
we walk in tongues,
cool-breezing down the pavement
like dusk in clean white
trainers and we smell like rain,
so everybody we pass looks
up with joy.

Graduates

Rain during the Paris leg was promised, but never came.
We reproached the host for calling us children
of colonisers, drank cooking wine and
waved passenger boats up the Seine.
We had no doubt beauties were alive in the world,
but knew we only existed in places like Wood Green,
Peckham Rye, Laurelton, Kensington Market, Half Way Tree.
We had travelled all over and never left anywhere behind,
being the kind of people for whom home can't be a place.
We went all around the musée, where the real
geographies had once been encased in glass.
Reparations have since emptied the palace, the tourists
taking photos of reflections of other tourists.

Manhattan Blue

Wonder, again, in a taxi. Baseball fans
flooding out of the stadium, a brilliance of blue,
even the driver wept. 7.34 a.m. in New York,
my head on your shoulder. At the stoplight,
the taxi driver asked where were we from?
Risk is a very welcoming country, I said,
anticipating the copper of our blood
in someone else's mouth. We asked where he was
from. He drew a line: the windscreen cracked
like a map. We saw the fields, charred buildings.
He said he wanted to visit our happiness.
We blew kisses into the blue jerseys'
hungry hallelujah. Radio played Billy Ocean,
we sang along, three freestanding hearts.
Day-thief windows over the tyres' ruleless
hush. We didn't notice the city's blue hours
climbing inside the cab. Avenues, burning like morning,
as expansive as teenagers on television,
we sang along because we were able to sing.
We moved closer, because.

Forrest Gump

Being twenty-one is like being lowercase god,
the cocky blue dress I wear at every party, the burning tree
in the wilds beyond my ends, supermarkets
at nighttime, the coolness of the light at dawn in an
    unfamiliar bed.
I play sad gay albums to a nub, summer grinds like a school
    dance.
I'm wise enough to know there are just two kinds of people:
girls with smudged mascara and girls with baby wipes.
July is as short-sighted as she is alive.
I can't get at love by swimming laps. I gather relics:
starry lipgloss, 7 a.m. glinting off running tapwater,
mismatched earrings, a lonely box braid on the subway.
Kindness is sharing jeans and deleting numbers.
The faces of strangers mean less and less.

Blue Pickup Truck

Every day there is less of you.
I had dreams about what lies I would
tell you, what classic cars we'd build.
My tits are shrinking, and we are back
to a lonely, clownish line. Beneath all these
bloody tissues is an albatross of wonder
but now the leather mitt's hollow, the umpire's called time
and I'm nobody's daddy in the baseball diamond.

Art of Water

Are there ways in which love is like water?
Am I like water? Am I cool girl or real cool?

There are currencies.
What parts of myself are we trading?

I will fold myself into a dream as transparent
as the architecture of my hunger.

People who walk over days like dreams
don't daydream, but aren't unlike me.

We suffer from generational anxieties –
everyone grew up somewhere, you know.

There's always a small town where you felt
like a sacrifice on unambiguous night streets,

wide awake to gossip twisting under streetlights.
Who isn't like love? We aren't only water.
We know enough about this world to summon its end.

Bas-Relief

Patient is most herself under threat of violence.
She moves easier than ribbon eels, like water
refractions under a stone bridge in the favela.
High spirits, in good humour, remarks:
a husband is just a man in your house.
Raise a fist and she becomes graceful
like a holiday, a housewife in a summer dress
with her back pressed to the light-
house, its guiding eye never falling
across her shade. Never revealing the deal
she's made. Being a ghost is delicious.
Nightmares: barrels of light, knives
in safe harbour. Certainty is a flat palm,
ringing ears. Storms are the presence of peace.
Look at what you love, then look at where you are.
Sadness and lust in bas-relief, dreams of turning men,
the lyre that wakes the sun, the honey, I'm home.

Kangaroo

Nights. September. Dusk.
Hills falling into a zoo enclosure,
train tracks cutting across rivers
like a sonogram's wand. I remember
        the first night we met
and you were crossing the street.
I was unfamiliar with capture then
but I would never be water, or sunbeams
in the leaves, just wind altering the surface,
just a poacher's shot whispering motherhood.

Alto

I watch nature documentaries, cancel the doctor's,
listen to Nina Simone 'til my skin turns blue.
The fair packs up for winter, I knead rosaries,
dunk paper wicks in urine with the religion of a rigged game.
Glaciers and species sink into extinction. I have appropriated loss.
Pearls running across my knuckles, mesh of a birdcage
veil brushing my cheeks, I confess: when I was fourteen
I joined the school choir to sing scales with a pretty alto.
We went swimming in our red cassocks, wet hair curling
like tongues folding over crispbread. We didn't need a word for
her hands pulling the white surplice over my head.
We pretended we shared the same escape routes, but
loneliness was easier for her to bear than punishment.
Whenever I prayed to be discovered, she kicked me under the pews.
I don't need to wonder if she has bled as extensively as I have.
At the spring fair I will eat cotton candy, ride the bumper cars
'til I appear in a rose window. There are all kinds of altars,
and there are just as many tables I won't ever name.

Green Parakeets

Are there as many green parakeets in your daydream universe as there are
in my daydream universe? Like the actress arriving at the train station in the rain,
I've been waiting for myself. What love means to the people who love me, I don't know.
Am I sad or ill-equipped? I close my eyes and it's just static. I want to be a sculptor's model,
neurotypical clay. I want to be sexy and profitable like a perfume advert or rivers
of streetlights, a Romantic language, a music video. I want to exist in a straight line.
Will you love me when I do not know how to love me, because I'm searching the platform?
I want to ask everyone, wrong answers only: do you need me the way I need me?
When I close my eyes it's glittering noise, non-native birds and tropical storms
mapping my limits, never striking the earth. One one thousand, two one thousand,
three one thousand, four.

Art Pop

Learning to drive in bare feet as a way to survive.
Blue jeans make you feel dishonest sticky
indiscreet. Stimming is just walking the pavement
at night repeating your favourite line
from your favourite scene. Whenever you're crying
you feel just human enough to sip rain or chew
green sugarcane in the heat like the corsage-wearing women
you wanna be kissing in strangers' backseats.
We're not winning any championship trophies
but it's always fascinating when you tell a new lie.
You're alive now but this used to be my playground.
Can't tell if he thinks you're talkative or just high.
At the visa counter
trying to explain what you mean when you say it's giving blue.
Walk slow, head down, a face in the crowd. We feel like magic
when we're acting: keep dancing, keep dancing.
What could be worse than social rejection? Dare you to
ask the moon if she knows she's just a reflection.

Love in the West

At the Langham, at the Mandrake, at the Shangri-La.
Retired psychiatrists, retired agency men, retired fathers.
Always a joke lurking somewhere, like a thin gold band
shaken free from his suit trouser pocket. Cried so hard
my teeth came loose, the client caught handfuls of bone.
He pocketed a couple. My insides felt like porcelain after.
Hairtie wrapped tight around the stack kept in the cobalt
lining of my overcoat. My heartbeat slowing on a comedown.
Noise of traffic rising from street level. A dance routine of doors.
Ease of a script. A back against a mattress is a familiar arc.
My opener was always, Are you a pig? Beat. Wink.
Beat. The client winks back, but the funny ones oink.

Water-Party (Taking Selfies)

With a manicured thumb underlining the title like a fish-
ing lure, I wait for the self-timer – clouds are clearing
for rush-hour traffic – it is dusk, atypical and golden –
yesterday was rent-day – I open to a random page – into
the midst of things: a woman – with an air of culture
and emotion – this chapter is about a lake party – who,
singing, belongs to life? who is merely swimming in bliss?
– outside the frame, I am watching that cartoon about a
carpenter's hubris – women in love are alive unabridged,
so far apart from the woman I am now – photographing,
very like the woman I normally am – at the big supermar-
ket and doctor's surgery, the art gallery – (unattended) – a
'whale' is a generous daddy – the blue fairy warns the boy
that life must be earned – she sounds like a person with
a net worth – this is where I first learned about love and
life, as animating qualities externally granted – do men
want a woman – in appearance – perfect and complete?
– I mostly want to be the girls escaping the party or –
slipping off the boat's roof – (I know my life belongs to
death) – but the whale opens his mouth wide and past his
hairbrush teeth, my wooden puppet boy waits for me – to
grow strings by the open flames.

Theory

Whatever I say or tweet – I am a short-sighted, emotional creature,
yoked to the economic relationships and material conditions
piling up in the street drains with balaclavas and crushed cartons of milk.
Every night is a cinderblock. We call this anti-intellectualism in some circles,
but what has not already been said? So many are outrunning faith.
So much falls right out of the sky. It's interesting we ever loved each other.

Lullabied asleep to police scanners beside campfires fed by national flags.
Monstrous – what can you expect of a birth on a deathbed? I read *Pedagogy*,
 I read Gramsci.

  I walk over the iceberg's forehead,

my footsteps shrouded with strangers' self-interest. I receive a great many direct messages.
I know what to think but not what to do. When I reach the city again, each train is rainbows
 and graffiti,

the precincts, ash in summer. Light passes through men like me, if I could even be called
a man,
if we could even call it light. It's the small labour we have been waiting for since grad school.

And we are so very happy watching the weeks burn, we can see so very far.

Bad Bitch on Her Best Behaviour

Deep down, I'm rain crystals and feathers.
Sugarbirds wonder about the deep pink:
Hottentot Venus is my ruling planet.

Oceanliners as theoretical shortcuts.
Husbands expect ambition from au pairs
and I want to prove you right.

Towards an ethnography of exposition:
pomegranate and American hysteria
come after white in the rainbow.

Chewing tobacco and candlelight,
grass skirts sewn by the zookeeper's sister.
Passivity and overcivilisation melt under my pussy.

If we speak only of black souls. The wind's hands,
burnished by our writhing. Say nothing of the physical.
What won't I do? What can't I do? 'I do not have limits',
myth? Way up high, I am wax, but you say I'll hold.

Outlaw Sonnet

I

Dear gorgeous artists:
stay inside, please! Criminals
like me won't spare you.

II

My daddy's vizier betrayed me, as I knew he would,
            the cowering scoundrel. We can't all be thieves.
The men in the camp grow rich and hungry, while I grow tired
            of heads on spikes. I want only beauty.

III

Without a brain or empathy! (A heart.)
An implication fattened by my hands and the dark.

IV

Dear ugly laymen:
the world isn't permanent.
Everything is ours.

V

Apologies and
crip theory over coffee.
An altar of spoons.

VI

Reaching a critical mass of diagnoses –
I keep living voluntarily, dressed in ruffs and diamond jacks.

VII

Fugitives, my worldly fugitives, steal whatever happiness
parades by you in the street. The world is a gala. Everything
is only forever when we die.

Ransom every kind of heaven and purgatory. Like, we'll still
die, but at least—

All the Birthday Girls

All the birthday girls at my birthday party
were stushy and mysterious. Beautiful gowns.
Communism was cool again, Instagram was attractive.
Students were in occupation. Sad boys were novelties,
sad girls aspirational. I felt very close to a legible version
    of myself.
I went to other people's parties without gifts
because I was the main character. That's youth!
Everyone felt like *someone*, I was still in love
with the city and protest chants and friends with money,
August evenings when the air smelled like hot rubbish.
Nollywood blockbusters in the braider's front room.
We drank palm wine, toasted baby girls and bootleggers.
At Sainsbury's I met a famous actor. I was on the till.
He was wearing a blue suit. I said it was my birthday.
The actor wished me Happy happy birthday darling
and bought a big bottle of champagne,
and took it away to someone else's birthday party.

Third Gender Sonnet

Everyone is female and everyone hates it.
    – Andrea Long Chu

Pop girls on the radio are singing about gender.
At the awards shows they are dancing gender.
On the silver screens they are playing gender.
In the high street shops they are buying gender,
drinking gender in the bars, kissing gender in the clubs,
reading gender on the bus to work, drawing gender on
the breath-frosted window with gender's own finger,
leaving the newspaper's front-page gender on the seat.
Landing on 'third gender' on the form with three tickboxes,
no write-in gender, then scribbling out this answer,
crossing out this umbrella gender entirely, picking a top hat
    gender
of the remaining two, incorrect genders, though not equally,
because this is where a third option leads us, gender escapees
    at a canyon
where our gender runs out of road.

Boob Jobs

are to Christmas movies what *Die Hard* is to gender affirmation.
This was never and always about sex. Re-articulating nerve
    endings
all weekend. Surgeons and forums talk about self-confidence
but what about body-mind integration?
Débutante desperado, there is no true self
except what we denounce, what we take
responsibility for. Wonder if our boobs need knife edges
in a society without inequity? Authenticity is not achievable as
    a state,
only an emotion, which passes like monopolies and
fashions, which are just monopolies of being. What about spirit?
Beauty ideals are like snowflakes. I wake up high on a gurney:
Yippee-ki-yay, motherfucker. Yippee-ki-yay.

Myth ~~of Old Age~~

Realistically, there will come a day when we're really really old, a day when we'll die. Thanks to modern medicine, we'll be old as balls. Thanks to future science, we'll know exactly when, we'll maybe even choose! We will have our eggs sunny side up and we will be wrinkly in a harsh, unrelenting way, because of the Botox. After breakfast we'll have really really great sex. One of my implants will go inside-out and we will both be cry-laughing. This will be an amazing, glorious day for us but maybe a sad, bittersweet day for everybody else who loves us alive. We will fall apart together, welcoming failing organs, fading eyesight, dimming voices. Some things will go with us. The things we forgot or did not want to pass on. With disuse, our names will float away into the atmosphere to join the cosmic junk orbiting Earth, the debris of chatter-less satellites and deserted spacecraft. We will wake that morning with the knowledge that we lived well: we made love in Wyoming and rescued witches in Mount Hagen. We lived on the same street for thirty years, we waited the same tables. I won the Nobel Peace Prize three times and at last learned to drive shift; your Grammy-winning triple-platinum album put all thirteen kids through school and allowed you to follow your dream of becoming an architect late in life. We will sneak past the orderlies on that shiny new day and abandon our clothes in the garden. We will run naked into the lake, laughing. When the kids arrive for our cool, damp bodies, they will probably not find any of it funny until the white sheet is pulled back and one of them will ask, Why are they naked?

Evening View of Twmpa
from Penybegwn

A clear, opaque sky.
Grass falling from my hair
like party streamers.
Lambs watch me.
We are all of everything.
your text messages to
me and mine to you.
Like a light on the hill,
I can see the future
of the world as its past.
From here, no enclosures.
From here, no wages or work hours.
From here, it doesn't matter
what you said or have not said,
what I wanted but didn't ask for.
I can see the beginning
and the end of this, the first time
we saw each other and
the last.

Wild Ponies

Why are everyone else's poems much more
perfect than mine? Very circular and cool
    with references, sexy with feeling!
I shouldn't think like this, but I want to do what bugs do
to a Michelin-star soup. Lights on the water are poets
laureate to the nightbus passengers. What a sudden voice
    in the peanuts means
to the deserted theatre. God, even wild ponies
    in a common field are rockstars to a walker. Both
builder and architect must be artists to the earth.
But there are green, wet feet in my work and I worry
the blank page gets tired of me. Reading stanzas through
    the wall I share with next-door,
all I see are my own knuckles passing over keys and ink
like dowsing rods. I am too familiar with my own poems.
Fine, I'll call these art. I'll call these my lovers. One day
    I'll accept the poet I am.

Kitchen at the Afterparty

I wish I was a walled rose garden – you know what I mean?
The guy whose house it is says, yeah,
I know exactly what you mean, sister.
He is not my brother,

                                  but I wish I was a walled
                                        rose garden

with a maze and a library at its centre.
                                  And the library is glass.
And the books are arranged by whether or not they're
any good. And there's always free desks and air-conditioning
because I am an exclusive member's club.
Not in a fascist wet dream kind of way,
but in a you-shall-not-pass-until-you-survive-three-spiritual-
    trials type of way.
Every person who crosses my threshold must tell me why they
    adore me,
and while it is not important that they actually do, I want to
    feel as though
they mean it.
                      And therefore I want to be a library of liars.
Where every book is just lie after lie after loving lie.
                            We're all lying down
on the parquet floor, me lying on the floor of myself,
tracking the movements of the sky through my own glass roof.
What a lonely library.
That's why all the books must be about what we don't have.
That's why it's always beginning to rain,
                         why it's almost morning.
I write so many poems about wanting

                                        you would think
all the ghosts had migrated by now,

                                        wouldn't you,
but there never was any light, there never was any tunnel.
Just a desperate people-pleaser of a library at the heart of
    a maze,
chalk-white arms reaching out of its hedges entombed by
    the flowering months
in the middle of the desert,
                    a failed exorcism of roses and lush green vines
pushing through the boundary walls like
            rivers of arrows firing from loopholes,
            like archers pulling bowstrings taut.

I close my eyes – nearer to prayer than I have ever been in
    a stranger's kitchen –
my-brother-not-my-brother listens like a sphinx.
        Yeah, roses.
Escaping through the brickwork, he says,
just trying to get the hell out of there.

Magical Girls

I am your only hope – the kindness of proverbial
strangers has been brought to its knees – discovered the
colour green the year we left the city, the year I learned
my first prayer – found it in a submissive sky, proof God
was really up there – chilling with the magical anime
girls – transformations to a colour-spectrum self – like
light in reverse through a prism, becoming a whole –
every high-schooler understands that we will need to save
the world – I knew this once too – at summer school I
listened to Stevie Wonder until all was really fair – until
war was green – everything we left began to return to
me – back then I was pure light – I was saved – (this was
the year I learned to kneel) – the logic of it was – the
kindness we withhold from ourselves, we do not extend
to others – the proverb was you – are my only hope.

Moon River

Party girls are art school drifters. Turquoise tea lights filled with menthol filters,
pink supermoons, social winters, huckleberry escapists with ankle blisters.
Fish in an aquarium, I browse the internet, I want to be vicarious. I want a new alphabet.

Video calls killed the celebrity class, we're progressing past the need for reality.
The slippage of time is its own tragedy, I can have any day of the week.
The air tastes braless when I'm drunk.

I feel sexier and sadder, like a tangelo or a cult classic. I wanna be mature,
wanna be dramatic. Age means I can't go home, it doesn't mean
I can't drink wine in the bath or vape alone. We all know a water sign
or a girl who loves tequila who's suffering especially.

We're living in screens, sick of neglect and numbers, we're toddlers with clever plastic toys,
can you hear the drummers? Reality's progressing past the need for us.

Sound and colour are more human, more universal than the electric slide, so
I listen to pop music with my friends and stream the sky.
Each morning is hot and blue, like a black-and-white movie.
Long, bright evenings twisting tighter than a scooby.

Teenage (Remix)

Hikers wish me illegal happiness.
We displace each other with a gaze,
the mobile signal hasn't recovered.
Cows, dying to know, press against the gates
as I walk past with my can of Guinness
harnessed like a baby, like a perfect world.
I take pictures of myself singing
and send them nowhere.
Maybe my life has surpassed me.
Everything is overgrown – pretend
icebergs aren't falling into the ocean today.
I reach the standing stones
and the ruins. I grew up here.

Cleaning Ladies I

And we scream on the way to work, fuck working! we're flirting with the future on the nightbus. Between this job and the next. Washing-up liquid and vinegar'll do the trick. The astronomical metropole lit up like winter. The villages, the realm of humans. Automatic, the hotel. Every body dismissible. Against the white neutral, killable. Employment is just a way to justify employers. We suspect you suspect of us a lack of interiority. Cardboard cut-out Western town of a girl. Wife without pearls. But everyone has a third life. You can tell who's comfortable to sit with a magazine while we work. Dirty thumbprints on the doorframe. Shit in the shower. Cigarettes in the freezer. Laundry line, designer dresses like bills on the breeze fluttering out of the blown-up cash machine. We see what you can't see. Train lights. Reflections sliding across unpolished silver. Caught holding the rag, fingers made of air. If you pay for the bunny suit, we'll clean in costume. If you pay for the language, we'll sing. Tidy away the debris of being alive so you can appear very alive. Lifts destined for even floors. Death by protagonism. Jeans from our twenties, failed sciences of being. Angel-eyed bioeconomic, we're the de-godded women. We're made of music, like birds. Like magic. Like the world perdu. Sad to have a view from somewhere, the unskilled under-privilege. Byproducts of education and empire. Ugh, the downstairs of it all. We charge our phone under the kitchen counter, but we don't have to drink your water. These are not your children. This is not your house. Is anything even playing in your earphones? The walk-in bathtub is a managerial class. The townhouse steps are an ecological threat. Let us go like a thousand pink party balloons. Paper lanterns labouring like the sun, when all the time your mother's earrings are under the bed. We know what you can't know. The P4 waits for no Man. Whatever happens, happens to you because of us. We own nothing in the world, just the world.

Acknowledgements

To my friends, my family. To my mum Marva, and my dads, Stanley and Stephen, always, always, thank you. To my sisters and brothers, to Josie. To Alexander, Daisy, Dill, Eliza, Ellie, Eve, Farrah, Franca, Georgia, Jack Smith, Jack Underwood, Khemi, Naomi, Sherrie, Steph and Susie. To everyone whose supported my work, especially Duriel, Durre, Dylan, Hanan, Joan, Louise, Nikesh, Taylor and Wayne. To the editors at *bath magg*, Gboyega, Joe and Mariah, who originally published 'Cowboy', and with whom I was privileged to work. To my agent Abi and the team at the Good Literary Agency. To my editor Martha and everyone at CHEERIO, thank you.

Thanks to the editors of the publications in which some of these poems first appeared: *Away with Words: Selected Verse, Volume 4*, *Bad Lilies*, *bath magg*, *The Demented Goddess*, *Lugubriations*, *LUMIN 3*, *Magma*, the *Oxonian Review*, *Prototype #1*, *Quirk*, *Vagabond City*, the *White Review*, *Y Stamp*. 'Art Pop' appears in the anthology *More Fiya: A New Collection of Black British Poetry*, edited by Kayo Chingonyi and published by Canongate. 'Cleaning Ladies II' was commissioned by *AZ Mag* as a short film.